GRAY WOLVES

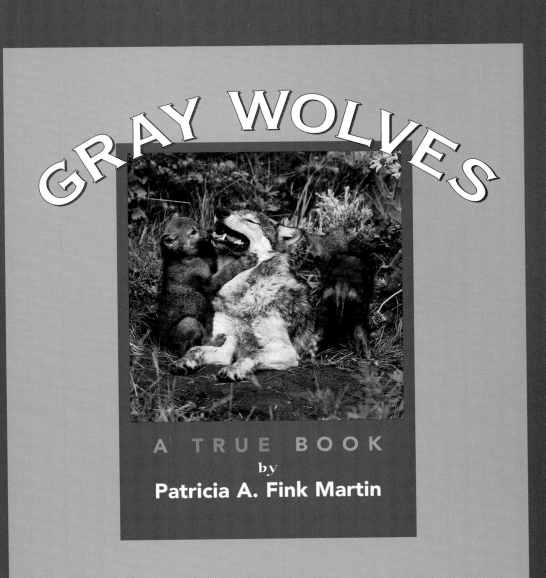

A TRUE BOOK

by

Patricia A. Fink Martin

Children's Press®
A Division of Scholastic Inc.

New York Toronto London Auckland Sydney
Mexico City New Delhi Hong Kong
Danbury, Connecticut

A gray wolf rests.

Reading Consultant
Nanci R. Vargus, Ed.D.
Primary Multiage Teacher
Decatur Township Schools,
Indianapolis, IN

Content Consultant
Kathy Carlstead, Ph.D.
Honolulu Zoo

Dedication:
To my daughter,
Leslie Sara Martin

The photograph on the cover
shows a gray wolf. The photograph on the title page shows
a gray wolf and her cubs.

Library of Congress Cataloging-in-Publication Data

Martin, Patricia A. Fink.
    Gray Wolves / by Patricia A. Fink Martin.
        p.   cm. — (A True book)
    Includes bibliographical references and index.
    Summary: Describes the physical characteristics, behavior, habitat, and
endangered status of gray wolves.
    ISBN 0-516-22162-0 (lib. bdg.)   0-516-27472-4 (pbk.)
    1. Wolves—Juvenile literature. [1. Wolves. 2. Endangered species.]
I. Title. II. Series.
QL737.C22 M3644 2002
599.773—dc21   2001032303

Contents

The King of Dogs

You may know some animals just by the sounds they make. Lions roar; owls hoot; wolves howl. But we recognize most animals by their looks. Would you know a wolf if you saw one? Not all wolves look alike. Some wolves have coats of white fur, while other wolves

This gray wolf has white fur.

have black fur. Most wolves
are covered with thick gray
fur, but some have red coats.

People often confuse wolves with coyotes or wild dogs. We've also given them many different names. Have you heard of a timber wolf, Arctic wolf, or Rocky Mountain wolf? Most belong to the same **species**, the gray wolf. This wolf once lived in North America, Europe, Asia, and the Arctic. A second kind of wolf, the red wolf, lives in the southeastern United States. However, most red wolves live

Even though gray wolves have different common names, they belong to the same species.

in zoos—only about eighty of these animals remain in the wild. Scientists place gray wolves and red wolves in the dog

Coyote

Red fox

family. Some other members of that family include coyotes, jackals, and foxes. All of these animals are built to run.

A wolf has a
pointed snout.

They hunt other animals and use their teeth as weapons.

The gray wolf is the largest wild member of the dog family. It weighs 60 to 100 pounds (27 to 45 kilograms) and is covered with thick fur. With its long legs, a wolf stands taller than a dog. Its eyes are golden yellow. A long, pointed **snout** sticks out from its face. Large, pointed ears sit on top of its head.

Big Ears

A wolf hears sound from far away. Its big, outer ears funnel sound to its inner ears. Humans also have outer ears but ours are smaller. Therefore, we cannot hear as well as a wolf can.

A wolf's external ears can turn in the direction of sound.

and Little Ears

Imagine if we had bigger outer ears. Would it improve our hearing?

Try this experiment to find out. First put a blindfold over your eyes, and then cup your hand behind one ear. Have a friend or a parent quietly move away from you and stop. Now ask them to drop a coin. Listen for the sound and point in that direction. Repeat the experiment without using your hand.

You can make an even bigger outer ear. Hold a piece of paper behind one ear. Listen for the sound of the coin as it hits the floor. Does it sound louder with your bigger ear?

Built to Hunt

Wolves were made to chase
and hunt their prey. To find
their food, they use their noses,
ears, and eyes. Even at night, a
wolf sees well. It looks for the
movements of an animal. With
its long snout, a wolf picks up
a scent in the wind or on the
ground. Its prey could be a

A wolf uses its eyes, ears, and nose to track its prey.

mile or more away. The wolf listens carefully. It can turn its outer ears to catch sound from any direction.

Once the wolf has spotted its prey, it begins the chase. Wolves run fast. They run well even in snow. Their big, wide feet keep them from sinking in the snow. A wolf's front paw can cover a 4-inch by 5-inch (10-centimeter by 13-centimeter) area.

To capture its prey, the wolf uses its jaws and teeth. Powerful muscles open and close its jaws. These jaws are twice as strong as those of a

Wolves run very fast,
even in the snow.

This wolf shows its long, canine teeth.

large dog, such as a German shepherd. A wolf also has special teeth in its mouth. Long, sharp teeth sit in the corners of each jaw. These **canine** teeth measure up to 2 inches (5 cm) long. With these teeth, the wolf grabs its victim. It cuts the flesh with smaller, front teeth called **incisors**. The wolf also has slicing and grinding teeth in its mouth.

A wolf uses its teeth to grasp its prey.

The Predator and Its Prey

Wolves don't always catch what they go after. Wolves often hunt large animals such as deer, moose, elk, and bison. Some of these large animals weigh more than 1,000 pounds (454 kg) and defend themselves with their hooves and horns.

An elk can fend off a wolf with its large antlers.

To kill such dangerous beasts, wolves hunt in groups made up of several adult male and female wolves. This hunting party doesn't often chase a

Wolves work together to track down prey.

healthy animal. Instead, it searches for weak animals that are old, sick, or very young.

The wolves first separate their victim from its group. Then they chase it to wear it out. A lead wolf sinks its fangs into the **prey's** back end or muzzle. The wolf soon pulls down the prey and kills it. The killer shares the meat with the group.

All the members of a pack share the meat.

The Wolf Pack

Wolves live with their hunting partners, and together they form a pack. In North America, most wolf packs contain five to ten wolves. But a pack isn't just a bunch of wolves—a pack is just another name for a type of family.

A wolf pack lives and hunts in a territory. Some territories cover

This pack has ten wolves.

only 20 square miles (53 square kilometers), but others may contain more than 800 square miles (2,000 sq km). Each wolf pack defends its territory from other packs.

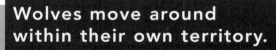

Wolves move around within their own territory.

Wolves keep the same mates for life.

An adult female and male wolf lead the pack. This pair stays together for life. Each year they have babies called pups. The pups form part of the pack. Last year's pups may live with the pack for a

Each wolf has a place in the pack.

time. The brother or sister of a lead wolf may join the pack too.

Wolves in a pack live by certain rules that help them stay alive. Each pack member holds a rank in the wolf family. Every wolf must know where it fits in. Scientists call the two lead wolves the **alpha wolves**. These wolves lead the hunts and decide when to rest. They eat before the others. In most packs, only they have pups. **Beta wolves** are next in line. Their job is to hunt and babysit. **Omega wolves** rank the lowest.

The alpha pair leads the other wolves.

Home in the Den

In most packs, the alpha pair mates in late winter. Before her pups are born, the mother finds a warm, safe place for her babies. She looks for space under an overhanging rock, or in a hollow log. She may even dig a tunnel into the ground. The place where she

This hole leads to an underground wolf den.

A young
wolf pup

gives birth and raises the pups
is called a **den**.

By the spring, a **litter** of four
to eight pups may be born. At

A mother feeds her pups milk.

birth the pups can't see or walk. Their mother feeds them milk and keeps them warm.

Pups crawl out of their dens and explore.

At three or four weeks, the pups crawl out of their den. For the first time, they meet their pack. They are greeted with howls and wagging tails. All members of the pack help raise the pups—they play with them, scold them, and teach them.

The pack protects the pups well. But soon they become adults and leave the pack. On their own, they search for food and mates.

Wolves in Trouble

Once more than a half million wolves lived in the United States. They hunted both small and large animals.

Some farmers and ranchers hunted the wolves because the wolves sometimes killed their farm animals. Farmers and ranchers hired gunmen to hunt

The number of wolves in the United States has decreased greatly.

the wolves down. These gun-men also put out poisons and traps for the wolves.

Early settlers came and set-tled many of the wild places.

Wolves cannot survive without wild places.

Wolves need wilderness. As the wilderness disappeared, wolves left. They searched out places where people didn't live. But our country is still growing, and fewer wild places survive.

Today only about nine thousand wolves live in the United States. Most can be found in the northern states. Special laws protect these animals. As an endangered species, the gray wolf may not be harmed.

Wolves are protected by law.

Saving the Wild Wolves

Many people want to see the gray wolf return to the places where it used to live. Wolves have already been brought back to Yellowstone National Park. In the Northeast, people plan to return the gray wolf to its wild places. Other places want wolves too. But some

Scientists bring a caged wolf into a
pen at Yellowstone National Park.

people oppose the plans. They
want to build houses, roads, and
hotels in the wilderness instead.
To save the wolves, however,

This scientist is putting a collar on a wolf to track it.

the wild places must be kept wild. Ranchers and farmers are also against the plans. They worry about the safety of their animals.

Wolves play an important role in the wilderness and we need

them back. You can help by telling others about them. You can also join a group that helps endangered animals and raise money for their projects.

Humans need to respect wolves so that they may remain a part of our world.

To Find Out More

If you'd like to learn more about the gray wolf and recovery programs, check out the following resources.

 **Books**

Beres, Samantha. **Wolf: Animal Savers: Take-Action.** Dutton Children's Books, 1999.

Brandenburg, Jim Scruffy. **A Wolf Finds Its Place in the Pack.** Walker and Company, 1996.

Dudley, Karen. **Wolves.** Raintree Steck-Vaughn Publishers, 1997.

Evert, Laura. **Wolves.** North Word Press, 2000.

Horton, Casey. **Wolves.** Marshall Cavendish, 1996.

Wexo, John Bonnett. **Wolves.** Wildlife Education, Ltd., 1998

Zeamen, John. **How the Wolf Became the Dog.** Franklin Watts, 1998.

Organizations and Online Sites

Defenders of Wildlife
1101 Fourteenth Street, NW
Suite 1400
Washington, DC   20005
http://www.kidsplanet.org

International Wolf Center
1396 Highway 169
Ely, MN   55731-8129
http://www.wolf.org

**National Wildlife
Federation**
1400 Sixteenth Street, NW
Washington, DC 20036
*http://www.nwf.org/nwf/
wolves*

Sinapu
P.O. Box 3243
Boulder, CO 80307
http://www.sinapu.org

Timber Wolf Alliance
Sigurd Olson
Environmental Institute
Northland College
Ashland, WI 54806-3999
*http://www.northland.
edu/soei/twa.index.html*

Wolf Park
Battle Ground, IN 47920
http://www.wolfpark.org

Wolf Sanctuary
P.O. Box 760
Eureka, MO 63025

Important Words

alpha wolf one of a mated pair that leads a wolf pack

beta wolf a wolf that ranks just below the lead or alpha wolf

canine a long, pointed tooth that sits in each corner of a jaw; a family of animals (the dog family) in which these teeth play an important role in hunting.

den a place where a mother wolf gives birth and raises her pups

incisor front tooth with a sharp edge

litter a group of young born of the same mother at the same time

omega wolf a wolf that ranks lowest in a wolf pack

prey an animal hunted by another animal

snout a part of the face of some animals that sticks out; it includes the nose and jaws

species a kind or type of living thing

Index

Meet the Author

Patricia A. Fink Martin holds a doctorate in biology. After spending many years teaching and working in the laboratory, she began writing science books for children. In 1998, *Booklist* chose her first book, *Animals that Walk on Water*, as one of the ten best animal books for children for that year. She has since published eight more books. Dr. Martin lives in Tennessee with her husband Jerry, their daughter Leslie, and their golden retriever Ginger.